Odd Botany

poems by

Thorpe Moeckel

Silverfish Review Press

Published by Silverfish Review Press
P.O. Box 3541
Eugene, OR 97403

ISBN: 1-878851-17-9

This publication was funded in part by a publisher's fellowship from Literary Arts, Inc. of Portland, Oregon.

Cover painting copyright © 1990 by Wolf Kahn.
Cover design by Valerie Brewster, Scribe Typography.
Text design by Rodger Moody and Connie Kudura, ProtoType Graphics.

Manufactured in the United States of America.

Acknowledgments

The author wishes to thank the following publications where some of the poems first appeared or are forthcoming.

Field: "Free Samples," "Late Morning in the Under-Atmosphere," "Now the Yellow Breeches," "Skink," "Poem with Braids in It," "Shout Out," and "From Monument Peak"

Poet Lore: "Bolin Creek" and "Orion the Hunter"

Cold Mountain Review: "On Field's Edge"

Potomac Review: "Thistle," "Pick-Up Game," and "For the Departure of the Kids I Was Supposed to Reform"

Wild Earth: "Meltlines"

Asheville Poetry Review: "At Courthouse Creek"

Salt Fork Review: "Why I Go to Bed Earlier" and "Sunday Evening at the School for Adjudicated Youth"

Free Lunch: "A Far Reach"

The Distillery: "On the Nature and Habit of Ants"

Mothering: "In the Basket Marty Brought to the Hospital After the Cesarean"

"Meltlines," "Muir," "Vespers," "On Being Eaten," and "From Monument Peak" appeared in a limited edition chapbook published by The Van Doren Company, Charlottesville, Virginia.

Thanks to Gary Young for choosing the manuscript, and to Aaron Baker and Rodger Moody for their editorial insights. I am grateful to John Towers, Charles Zartman, John and Beth Frumer, and Mike and Lucretia Woodruff for shelter, land, and good company during the writing of this book. Thanks also to Franklin Burroughs, Tony Hoagland, and Kenneth Rosen for early guidance, and to the faculty and students at the University of Virginia.

Many thanks as well to the Jacob K. Javits Fellowship of the U.S. Department of Education for financial support, to Peter Relic, to the Tressler Wilderness School, and to my family for their love.

Contents

Part I

Part II

for Kirsten

Part I

BARTRAM'S TRAIL

To follow Bartram's trail upstream, past Tugaloo,
to cross the Chattooga River at Earl's Ford,
to go up the Warwoman Valley,
up past the cascades & bridalveils of Finney Creek,
up along the Continental Divide
between Rabun Bald & Hickory Knob,
is to crawl, is to hopscotch
between the doghobble and the yellowroot,
the rhododendron and the laurel, hand over hand,
inch by dirty, glistening inch;
to follow Bartram is to squirm, prostrate,
under the lattice-work of limb,
the umbrellaed variations of lanceolate,
the way the lungless slip like tongues
through the tiny, moss-flamed grottoes,
oblivious to four-legged jesuses
walking on the water's white-lit roostertails;
to follow Bartram's trail is to go
wet-socked, knee-weary & briar-inked,
is to limbo under shadows
mosaiced and three-quarter domed;
to follow Bartram as far as the end
is split, past the leastmost echo,
past the hiccup of wild mint and galax,
the azalea, the teaberry, the trailing arbutus;
to follow Bartram into the shade of the giant poplar,
across the intersection of trunk and root,
across the blighted chestnuts,
is to find the place
where no pattern goes unrepeated,
the place where the first ashes were spread.

A FAR REACH

Along boulevards
of cohosh and ground cedar,

where ice once carved,
when the sun was a far reach

through the milkweed
of the clouds,

we walked. Everywhere
the low, shade choked limbs

of the white pines
crowded the woods

with their delicate scaffolding,
and sometimes the dogs

tore through the lowbush and broad beech fern
after a whiff,

their tongues tremendous
and thick with drool. Remember

how the birch, moss-frosted & shaggy
with unpeelings,

clung to the ledge, white
as brides,

how the mushrooms withered
in the duff, & the indian pipe,

that swan-elegant parasite,
came up between

the deadfall and the stumps.
Remember, dear, how the wood thrush,

one brook and stone wall away,
played its undulant

flute-wind, and how, like happy fools,
we tried to sing along.

SUNDAY EVENING AT THE SCHOOL
FOR ADJUDICATED YOUTH

Lilac clippings in a Dixie Cup,
Sammy Kershaw on the White-Westinghouse,
the phone in front of me dying
to be dialed, touched, talked to — Sundays
come quick, & I sit in the ruins

of another weekend shift, one ten
& two fifteens, the hours a slow
hemorrhaging; boys in the day-room
eating Granola Bars — "particle board,"
they call it — and telling lies.

Already the toilet's clogged.
Already Tom has filed a grievance on me
for making him crap outside
in woods made gothic by rain
& rain's unborderings. I document

what I know & more what I don't, counseling
a kind of fiction, a kind
of autobiography. Soon night-shift
will relieve me. Soon the boys will
squirm in their bunks, having hit

the lotion-stash for a date
with Rosie P. For now, Sammy Kershaw
goes on, number sixteen on the countdown, & outside
another April dusk falls, ennabling
whole anthologies of smudge.

HOMAGES

I want the trees lined up between the fields to be trees
today, not show girls, not antlers, candles, or scarecrows
pointing the way to OZ; I want the curves of their limbs
to be the curves of their limbs, not filigree,
not fingers, spines or necks, not wishbones,
no orchestra of held postures —
no demi-plié, downward dog, or salute to the sun.

I want the trees to be trees, wood,
softwood, hardwood, burled & broken, deep-rooted
& full of bitter syrup — phloem, xylem —
not fine grain, no medullary rays, wood floors,
keels, or axe-handles. No likes, the ways,
just as, or as ifs, I want

the trees to be trees, winter trees,
planted forty or sixty years ago,
by some lucky fool with a luckier tune
in mind and the promise of hot German pancakes
keeping the heartaches at bay. I know
how agony can become a form of ecstasy

one revels in, day upon day, but I want
the bark to be bark, not armor, not felted wool,
I want what's left of the severed limbs
to be what's left, not coat-hooks, pitiful
& phallic-looking, and let's not load down
the bittersweet & muscadine vines
with action verbs — those aren't

lines of black ink doodled on a curdled sky;
the few remaining leaves are the few
remaining leaves, not rust, not brindle,
not paint thumb-flicked from toothbrush bristle,
the way you did in your landscapes,
your homages to Wyeth; and this, Pop Pop,
Andrew, you old barred owls, is all I can do.

SHOUT OUT

This is a shout out to the only rap show
this side of the Susquehanna, a shout out
to P-Man for mixing Nas with Wu-Tang,

the new one by the Gravediggaz
with Tupac, 'Lil. Kim, & Biggie Smalls.
So props to the records, stacked like mica,

the CD's diesel and sedimentary on tables,
speakers, floors; props to the haywire
of input, output, knobs that slide,

dial, click; props to the flyest,
bombest, off the hookest sampling
of ghetto life in this cowpatty on fieldstone

of a town; mad props
to the requests pouring in,
props to the white bread farm kids,

the Army War College kids, to all
the relocated sons and daughters who
white, black, pink, green wish they were blacker,

who dress up in Timbs, Tommys, DLO, Fubu —
citified fatigues — all the blow
blowhards who are afraid & therefore

not afraid to puff a blunt & get hype,
who aren't urban but have urban hormones,
have 14-year-old beeper-wearing, AK-toting,

crack-selling pipsqueaks for hormones
marketing the latest in down-n-out attitude, the newest
in pseudo-revolutionary, consumer-as-gangster fashion

through the shopping malls
& Yo MTV Raps of their veins;
peace out, kid, for real.

AT COURTHOUSE CREEK

Check out the hemlock, heavy & atwitch
with the steady, fat-lipped rain
on river left, halfway up

Salvation's spiral staircase,
its needles feathery & beatboxed,
nothing's eyelashes, nothing's pulp;

check out the treetrunks, gnarl-fingered
& strophic, between the sweet pepperbush
and the rattlesnake plantain, the brook trout

beneath the convergence of two wave trains
and an eddy's ass-end, where
the glare's blueberry-banana,

cross hatched & curlicued; check out
the creek's coastal range,
its lake region, tundra, & Lava Falls,

its Chinese characters, sea stacks,
grocery lists, jobs with benefits;
check it out, how the birch limbs

wedged by highwater in the damp dark
amongst hellbender & hellgrammite
point to Heaven's ten thousand

four-way stops. Change is light:
watch it, watch the sun's lurid monologue,
thoughtless, time-splashed,

top dead center; watch it,
leaf-filtered & on the move, blister
the water's errant flecks.

ON FIELD'S EDGE

Late October is a hard time
if you're used to living in the woods,
used to hiding out in the hemlocks,
in the mountain laurel & ferns,
taking your walks, finding your footholds
where the hawks couldn't see you,
where the airplanes were a grey noise above the trees;

a hard time if you're used to looking down on all of this,
the cornfields, locust-groves, the gridwork
of asphalt and rail, the twin silos,
twin tin-roofed barns, the land
shaved clean; looking down
from the Blue Ridge, South Mountain,
from Center Point Knob;

a hard time if you've never lived in the flatlands,
on field's edge, never lived where clouds bounce
their steel hulls on the blue tides, where the wind
takes long, bold brushstrokes, and crows fishtail above
the fenceline, above the walnut's candled limbs,
like peepholes to the lands you've loved,
the lands you've left behind.

A FEBRUARY INDULGENCE

First smoosh the bittersweet,
mash tinctures of pokeweed stalks,
umber, mold-imbued, odor
of hot armpits & cold feet.
Infuse gourd-skin in manure-juice,
in the dismembered mourning dove's
catbriar-colored
feather-soup. Pound up walnut,
grind quartzite
with roadkilled-opossum tooth.
So the palette seethes. For the fine lines,
lash one spine
from the blackberry stalk
to the end of a hophornbeam twig, a live,
sleeping one. But there are no
fine lines, so chew
wads of locust bark, then hawk bits of it,
eviscerated, to resemble
what fissures of leaf
& last year's grass emerge
from the puny cirques of ice.
Blend smoothies of owl scat & pond scum,
then fingerpaint the fudge swirls
of vine on fencepost, or gleeck
lugies of deep-sinus snot,
of intellectual jock itch
& other stray brain stuff,
infected & carp-tongue green off
the cracked desert of your lips,
but don't call it mixed media,
don't call it full body collage,
call it living, call it
getting by.

CHATTOOGA

You don't know how the aluminum pole will feel on a body that's been underwater for three days, and you don't quite trust that you can tell the difference between flesh and wood this evening as you poke and probe from a raft platform in a rapid paddlers call Jawbone. All you know is the color of the water matches its sound and there is a wolf spider on every rock you use for balance and there are men on the bank, kin to the boy, with pistols and machetes and they claim to have killed fourteen snakes. You don't know that in seven days the boy will surface in an eddy where a raft trip — yours — has pulled over to eat lunch. And you have no idea that your friend three years from now with a grappling hook and come-along will unwedge a college student from the slot below Left Crack, don't know he'll have to wait a week for the river to drop, that even then with the force of the water, the body will only come in pieces, and that when you ask him about it — it's amazing what we remember — he'll say the watch on the left wrist was still ticking. And of course you don't know that in five years, in the same year and month that a doctor will cut your first born from your wife's belly, a man will lose his daughter in Raven Chute, that after weeks she won't surface, and that he'll attempt to dynamite the river, try to break its jaw so he can recover her body, so he can bury her proper. This evening with the aluminum pole growing colder in your hands and the men on the bank starting fires, some coiling rope, you don't know what you know, what you're feeling, don't know that even if this man five years from now finds his daughter, some part of him will have to leave her there and walk into the water below Raven Chute, just downstream where it's almost calm, walk in for as long as is needed — maybe a whole life — walk in every day, and bathe.

FERN

Carboniferous one, coal's secret agent —
your fruit dot is in the cirrus today,
and though I'm trying to live like that,
mulitudinous, wired to send roots, connect,
I know you used to be massive, tree-sized,
and would have feared seeing you then —
Paleozoic skyscraper — standing in your shade,
unable to blot you out with a step,
the way I do walking these drainages & slopes,
worrying your particular names,
cinnamon, ostrich, maidenhair —
because you don't flower, you don't flower —
how they're entwined & bring me closer
to your center, that slipperyness: earned grace.

KILLDEER

Father yelled "bird in the field,"
and though I saw its wings were longer & sharper-hooked
than the mourning dove's,

his voice was bulletproof, deader serious
than when he left
the head of the dinner table

to fire at the solicitors
another, "we're not interested." So I moved
his twenty gauge in front of the killdeer

and sent the bundle of feathers
on an airborne slam dance
with the red clay dust. "That was a tough shot,"

he said, but when his hand
squeezed my own
I was not his good son, I was

the hollow
bones that allow birds flight,
I was a bluegill

thrown back
with a treble hook
still deep in its throat.

FREE SAMPLES

East of Asheville, rush hour, I-40, August
sun a warm feather pillow; deep-squint
as we pass the Biltmore Oil truck

at seventy-five; Blue Ridge
a regular EKG above the highway's
skidmarked corridor,

green as we approach it,
green as we go away.
God bless input:

mullein, joe pye weed, queen anne's lace
as if the guardrail was put there
to keep them lined up

below the sweetgum's limp, lace-cuffed wrists,
the catawba's fat green junkmail. God bless
the empty basketball courts, netless rim

on telephone pole, red clay
cracked and weed-patched. God bless
the runaway truck ramps

as we leave Pisgah National Forest,
and come into furniture country
— life's free samples —

burning brake pads, Sue's fingers,
like smilax, on the van's wheel,
loose, long, and unfailing;

snuffaluphagi of kudzu, shudder of sedge;
silent but deadlies in the back seat,
and alphabet races, B-bridge, C-grace.

POEM WITH BRAIDS IN IT

No more consonants, now, the alphabet
is pure vowel, and geese
waddle west in this mud,

this soft serve, opening their wings
now and then, as if to say,
in their aloey jargon,

who's boss. Already
a balmy phonics descends; the locust blossoms,
those pea-shaped buggers, those

millennium falcons, swim
through its trickster palette, looking
for the tea in which the world steeps,

in which noise
chases noise through lives
haunted by new flaws, new flaccidities

and an honest, down-
to-earth rain. Meanwhile, up-country,
between the oaks,

the ostrich ferns offer their ancient scrolls
with flimsical precision,
& Little Dogwood Creek braids

its bubbly logistics, pummeling
the azalea clean
as sleep, or the impulse

to reveal the impulse
by running from it. Here's
to the basket-weave of the greenbriar.

Here's to the indian cucumber's split-level rendering
of starfish. Here's to the tumbledown acoustics,
the caddisfly, the constant

participling. Here's
to the carnal life, the leaves
folded like dozing bats.

PAWLEY'S ISLAND SHAKEDOWN

Today the light heals
and so does the dark.
Today we change
despite ourselves.

Thresholds appear
along the high tide line
by the driftwood and the abandoned boogie board.
See the wind, from the west,

comb the surf's white hair back.
Downbeach, an osprey turns olympian rings
above the sand-flats,
above the shrill-green bands of spartina.

Downbeach, barnacles of sun pop
off the inlet
like grits on fire.
See the chased minnows' quicksilver.

See the brown scum fiddlehead on the eddyline,
as the tide goes out,
as the marsh gives up its loot.
See it again and again

and again, in the surround sound of cicada and wave,
before the spread of tide-scalloped sand,
catamaran masts at eleven o'clock,
palmettos in fruit, swallows

darting above the green scissorhands of the leaves.
There's no horizon,
no line on the Atlantic
as if the world was flat,

just the glare and the shine,
just human figures walking,
and the footprints of ghost crabs,
and the glare and the shade and the shine.

THISTLE

I prefer, dear thistle,
to gnaw my sorrow
in the prodigal origami
of your shade. It comforts,

those puff pastry blossoms,
the odd cartilage
of your travertine leaves.
It comforts how you up

the ante. Deviant mimosa,
asparagus with attitude,
I love how you reach
through the romance

of my blue jeans; how,
like a beauty the world
fought with all its mind
to ignore, you come up

along the unmown edges,
red-fanged & fraggle-rocked:
grief's state flower,
desire's boutonniere.

BATIK

To learn the vernacular of a land
that's never known frost,
you do what you must: let the color blue
snorkel through the rebellion of your eyes;
accept the sun, the equatorial sun, as a song
you can't get out of your head;

walk through the language like a stranger
alienated from your stride, trip
on the organ pipe, feel the tamarind
comb out the wind's nattiest dread. Here
the trails are as steep as the stripes
on the anole's back, and you
hang your towel on the manghineel,

hitch to the tarpon's dorsal fin,
and sit in an outhouse, on the East End, listening
to soldier crabs — esoteric scavengers —
get fat in the pit; you go
at dusk, while the sailboats roll in their sleep, white
on the sullen torquoise,
while one butterfly flitters

along like desire's altargirl, and hear
the booby's eighteen dialects of Old Dutch;
you stand in the aroma of bay leaves,
St. Thomas to the west
like a loaf of old moldy lava, sunlight
adrift on the clouds' fringing reefs,
and as the crushed coral turns

on the ratchets of the waves, let
sand fleas sip red rum in the shade

of your sugar factory. Here the water
behaves at the mouth as it does
at the source, and you better
believe the pelicans like the fish
more than the impact, especially

the jack — piscean gangster — who wears
welder's glasses and an umber suit, the one
who's as tall as long and sports
a sleeveless neon-mauve pin stripe
to intimidate the yacht-shaped barracuda, the one
who loves how the hawksbill
flies in on its front wings

like a banished bird, its shell
beehived, flies where the sun, filtered, makes
fuzzy lines of batik on sand-ridge,
on labyrinthine brain coral, on the deep purple fan
that sways as if laughing, tourist,
at the hilarity
and redemption of your estrangement.

ORION THE HUNTER

To work tomorrow I will wear my thickest socks
and say of my slight limp that I walked
for miles, that I spent the weekend up north,
in the wilds, tracking whitetails, that I hunted

until my feet began to bleed. For now
it's all-skate at the Midway Roller Rink,
the Spice Girls are on, and I'm cruising
through the nacho-cheese smell, clockwise,

on rentals, against the sterling grain
of the the disco ball, hot spots
forming on the arch of my feet like
reminders that I'm human, that I'm

the choices I can't make, that next
to *maybe*, my favorite word is *or*,
and *need* is just that, a fucking verb.
Four wheels, boots laced up high,

I love how the floor guards slow down
the reckless, love how the bra-straps
bulge on the tight halter tops. Someday
I might do the hokey pokey, might

put my left foot in & turn myself around,
but God the curves come quick; I take them
like the years, deliciously, obliviously,
in camouflage and a blaze orange vest.

PICK-UP GAME

Mather Gorge, Potomac, Virginia side,
and between the armored cars
of dolomite, the bands of quartz,
faulted folds, & other testaments
to geologic trauma, lie fairways of three day old snow
like glaciers in miniature, grainy,
granular, & clinging to the moss
& lichen's dense pinchushions, cauliflower-eared,
stop-frame sculptures of the river
where it spritzes in low
January sunlight through syncline & anticline,
spritzes and splats as if Arthur Dove's oils
on canvas got up and left
the Phillips Collection, disgusted
by so much gawking, got up
along with Gaugain's "Still Life With Ham,"
& booked, jetted only
to recongregate here under the chessboard
of cloud and sky, in this pick-up
game of ice, shadow, and light, safe
from the cultivated gaze, the silent
conniptions, safe & in cahoots
with their psychic brethren, here,
where in a corner pocket
of metasedimentary conglomerate,
the dwarf cypress, tree of lowlands,
thick heat, live moss, tree of the Ogeechee,
Seminole, Okeefenokee, hangs on
by its Yankee-most roots.

FOR THE DEPARTURE OF THE KIDS
I WAS SUPPOSED TO REFORM

Today, the last, creeps up
on the deep August woods. Dawn
lays in its hammock, unworried
and back-lit; yesterday's raindrops
like crystal ticks on the poplar's

hound ears. It's hard
knowing I won't see you again,
knowing that it's time to say goodbye,
when we've hardly said hello, but
doesn't the connection begin

after the farewell, the way
learning begins after we graduate.
Twice, in the last thirty days,
I've realized what I'm doing here,
and I'm not convinced

it'd be nice to forget how to forgive
because we didn't need to,
I'm not convinced
facing one's conscience,
is any kind of acupuncture for the soul.

But didn't you love the sound
of leaves drying off, the morse code
of raindrops downclimbing
the leaf-ladder, the waterstriders
going one Mississippi, two Mississippi

under the bridge, the brocades of silk,
the daddy-long-leg-soup, and the ferns,
the ferns, primordial
and bent
under their own green weight.

Part II

ROPETHROWS

Though my grandfather never came rafting,
Pop Pop made a watercolor
from a photo of my father, brother, and me
in a four-man at Woodall Shoals,

and he always asked about the work
and all the other hopelessly heroic jobs
he probably didn't approve of
as if he'd start them tomorrow

with nothing except what he'd heard; he
knew, for instance, how at the big drops
we set rope in case rafts dumped,
to stop swimmers before the next; knew

we parked in safe eddies, had guests
wait (they dreaded & loved the suspense),
then took a coil and a bag,
and hustled to set up; knew it was

best to rockhop barefoot, or wear
sandals of hemprope, believing each step
was the one, and pushing off
the chipped tooth of schist, a leap

over crevice and already looking
for the next. *Pace is place,*
Pop Pop said, a fact he knew
from painting, how everything moves —

trees, even stone — after looking
at water so long. He liked that some guides
practiced their throws and others
felt it jinxed them, and nothing worse

than a missed throw except laying
the rope across a swimmer's chest
then letting go, or getting dragged in
as I was yesterday in the nursing home

when wanting like in some gospel
a rope from heaven to save us
not from death so much as loneliness,
I held the thin, liver-splotched braid

of his hand, and knew no rope
could help but a river was
a rope with no end only a loop
of knots in sky earth flesh sun,

and tried not to cry and even harder
as from within the steely cavern
of Alzheimers, Pop Pop said,
it's nice to meet you.

FROM MONUMENT PEAK

Alaska Range, molared & calcitic, all drainage
& archetype — auroras of lichen
                              blister the scree,
        off-shades, staccato & stucco,
nothing but fragments, talus slopes,
                    heath hunkered in.
            Even the Wood River —
no wider than my finger —
uncoils,
                        flush & gravelbar,
part download, part shoulderblade,
            a parabola, a cutting through.
Lord, the erosion is everywhere,
                        the distance always near:
ponds brood in the muskeg,
                    permafrost two feet under. Shut
your eyes, sleep on it.
The sun's countersunk,
                    all flute & bone,
            and I can hear the hymns of old miners
in the wind, chased with curses.

MUIR

Embosomed, wrote Muir of the Coastal Range
as if nursed on the slow milk of glaciers.
How they calve along sutures, carving, grinding —
a massive, crepital shift; grit, algae, old snow,
huge & plastic, a life of ice worms, puddle-fever.
How desire with its low pay, its overtime
refuels there, at the eros of confluences,
where resistance is reverie & along the moraine,
a constant re-ordering: meltlines, the music
of slipstreams, wind in the hollows, cloud.
Surely his mother rocked him wild & hard
those nights in Wisconsin, or not at all.
What else could he say in that place?
Embosomed, he wrote, sixty feet up a sitka spruce.

ON BEING EATEN

The curt savagery
            of her paw
        plows my spine. I hear
a magpie; it sounds
                    too neutral. On my knees
                        there's a stone,
            I chunk it, hoping
to meet skull, & hard enough,
                            but there's a light
        so bright I know
it's over. I know without
                    having to be told.
            I won't be told,
because I'm lupine, because
        she's found
the omelet
                    & is rubbing her neck
in my guts
        as if perfume. Know this:
                        there's ecstasy
            in death, and some days it moans
your name,
                it claws & it moans.

MELTLINES

The clouds are wedges of peach, salmon
running. They brood
and swell,
distinct, now indistinct

above the valley whose
walls slough
in great fans
of talus & scree. Upriver

the light walks on its hands,
feeling the water's pulse. Evening
is clouded emerald,
tungsten. Here

the continent reinvents
itself each day; I become
what the glacier lets
go of, and what

it takes along,
nothing but lines, long
and broken,
that connect even

as they tear away,
of sediment, drainage
& horizon,
and the shapes

within, an emptiness
and a comprehension —
how at home
my bones

feel here, future
a nibble of rain
on the neck, the river
swirling me in its mouth.

WHY I GO TO BED EARLIER

Nothing undoes the knot behind my chest
more than watching you take off your clothes
before bed. Eyes on the floor, wall, or window
as if some swath of dust helps you remember
its the blouse Ruth left last March,
the underwear you wore to graduation,
the bra you'll go to India in. It gets real
halfway between my bellybutton & spine,
and sometimes I lie there pretending to read,
book hardly below my eyes, your weight
balanced on one leg — a live oak — torso,
shoulder, and neck bent as your arm
reaches, your knee rises, and your thumb
peels the ripe, white fruit of your foot
out of the sock. Then, in forty watt dark,
I love your cold skin, as a wick
takes flame from a match, and gives it
time, sweet time, to burn and shine.

THE OYSTER GATHERER

for John Towers

He dances the flats, gleaner of tides
in yellow knee highs, snatches
the creatures that spit & cough, rugged
razors of lavender, sphagnum, peach —

throws out the sprung ones,
mudders, black hearts sliding
into rockweed, kelp, & knotted wrack.
Each winter, when the Gulf

bottoms out, he goes, salt-licked
& nerve-numb, legs tireless reeds —
sea ducks further out
towards Winnegance, the sun

low & glowing off vacant
summer homes. It's work,
the way love is, being a friend,
building a house,

or after the shucking, chopping
garlic & lime. He's learned
to see past reflections —
birch, white pine, sky —

to mud & clay, what's there.
Now the clatter & drainage
of his perforated spackle bucket
filling up: listen, listen.

WHITE

It is the same white as pipsissewa,
nodding flower of barren acidities;
the white of the ground beneath
the eagle's nest; the white of indian pipe,

defiance and its consequence;
the white between the dear and the amen;
the white of a moth's wings, and the smell
in the morning, down by the logjam,

under the hemlocks, in that ghetto
of green, where light and moving water
are continuously wed; the bridal white,
white of fungus, surrender, the abyss;

the white of the fifth syllable
in the idea and the meaning of the idea,
the soft, unaccented one
white neither sulks nor rejoices behind.

IN THE BASKET MARTY BROUGHT TO
THE HOSPITAL AFTER THE CESAREAN

Asparagus-pasta cobbler; raspberry bread; fresh
baked whole wheat bread; collages

young Molly did
on construction paper — de Kooning-esque —

with catalog clippings, great swirlies
of magic

marker, & filaments of glitter-laced glue;
Parmesan-mushroom wild rice;

boxed pear juice, boxed mixed fruit juice;
soy milk; mangoes; cold

cucumber-yogurt soup; fresh strawberries;
cut lilac; blackberry tea;

a hand-turned ceramic vase; a doll
sewn of scrap fabric, of stuffed athletic sock;

and a bouquet of herbs: fresh
mint, fresh rosemary, freshest sage.

VESPERS

Late-morning
    on the far side of the river,
        & from an EZ-chair of moss,

I'm starting to believe
    in the world again. Spruce trees,
        spaced out & arthritic, are candles

longest winter
    can't extinguish. Here
        are shrubs with scallops

for leaves, serrated rose.
    One golden eagle
        is a mote above Anderson's long

east flank. Everywhere
    a smorgasbord of impossibility —
        chatter of waxwing

& ground squirrel, high slopes
    varnished in copper,
        iron, coal. Now the wind

brings vespers
    from the rivers of ice
        below Denali; how audible

are the consonants
    & hard E's, the sh — Kantishna, Tatshenshini —
        how permanent & how real beneath my feet.

SLOW RIVER PURPLING

Not bright so   much as purpled
pressure-washed   the heart's headlamp
is on licking   everything even

the banks   hovering so many
holes without   bottom deeper
than the river   they shuttle that
with some rain   more rain gouges

its throat that   once breathed
dew once floated   hulls of splottled
paw paw its veins   home to minnows

that'll never   become fish
don't care to   See the tanninfoam
Matisse scissorwork   the algae denser
than figs scrotal   awaft O heart

wet heart how   many geographies
can one cubic   inch contain Ask
the bubbles ask   the spawn

LATE MORNING IN THE UNDER-ATMOSPHERE

The treetops are nowhere, as insignificant
as an idea,
and life-affirming. But, to the east, stretched

between the trunks of two persimmon trees —
ragged juveniles —
a spider is spinning another groove

in its 33, clockwise threads
concentric with the web's midpoint,
its bullseye, now you see it,

now you don't. Light's funny — sometimes
the thin, dartboarded segments
of 12 & 6 o'clock

are a fuzzy gossamer rainbow color;
sometimes there is only the black triangle
of the spider, going around,

before the immense spreadeagle
of green, like a second-hand
with no arm, like a thing

with nothing better to do. Below,
in the morning's groundswells,
in the displacement of the yellowjackets

& bottlefly's fast wings,
in that stepped-on & overlooked atmosphere,
alive with thermals, microbursts,

twelve thousand dramas and
undiscovered genres, a daddy long legs,
its body more acorn fragment

than pentagon reject,
waits its turn
to dismember a katydid, waits

behind a red ant
to tear from the katydid's wing
or abdomen,

a scrap, a nickel-bagged
piece of cargo
too heavy to go far with.

BOLIN CREEK

I think of the bream in your red clay shallows,
their olive-hued longitudes
and copper breasts, their
huge pupils & the way
they squiggle,
like thoughts, or desire, nowhere
according to nothing
determinable;
I think of their silence,
how mushroom clouds of silt rise
where they brush rock or limb;

and of your undercut banks, how, along them,
amongst sphagnum and spleenwort,
several trees rise from one
system of roots, at
the sun's favorite angle;

of the wild ginger
along the root-studded footpath,
the cedar, umbrella magnolia,
gifts of the sycamore;

the rhombozoids & parallelograms of bedrock,
and how, in June, in the stagnant runs, as if
the eye contained all the heart

did & did not know about love,
there's the bottom
of one hundred leaves to look at,
ironwood leaves, reflected
in a chain-link configuration, top lit
& unctuous like
accidental filigree – I think of that,

and of the cicada's trill crescendos
in the brain-dead afternoons, and the dogwalkers
conversing, and the sound
of mountain bikes — squeal of brake pad on rim —
coming through the hardwoods and the pines.

LIVING BY WATER

How many times can a man go to the river,
dip his hands in, touch them to his face,

face the wind, the sun, then touch the rocks
so as not to fall stepping across,

scrambling to a certain beach or grotto
where in going, in arriving, in every breath

between, the heart sheds foul layers —
greed, vanity — as if shale, the flakes

worked by gravity to sand, mineral –
water he spits, water he thirsts for;

how many before he's holding the hands
of children, keeping them from falling in,

knowing they must, as a river must
not make a circle nor a man too easily believe

in rivers, no matter droughts known,
obscenities of flood, choking trout,

bloated fawns; no matter how many boats
pushed off – boats of sin,

redemption-boats – or bodies explored,
campsites slept with sounds of water

tucking behind every rock burst against;
how many before he must be carried there,

perhaps by a stranger, perhaps he's the stranger now,
but not to the birds, beasts, flowers because

he's forgotten their names, knows they were
never grateful of his awe, less of his pity.

PAPA BOAT BIG WAWA

was your first sentence,
a sort of reference, having watched me drive off
with a canoe on the roof.
But those two weeks
apart — January, days of snow, ice —

I did not boat. Craving someone
to hold, or hold me — I wrote, rode rivers
of language, while we struggled,
your mother & I, to unravel our marriage's turgid syntax —
what will I do, what do I need,

want, you, me — pronouns
crossing borders. In between
homes, waiting for tiles, a new
coat of paint, mother & you
with Omi & Opa, four hours

south — letters came & went,
and because a new house
is a new phase & demands
a kind of watershedding, each day
we walked the telephone's frozen lake,

our words deliberate, dying
to break through, as you did, standing there
holding the window, all
noun & verb — *papa boat,*
bye bye, papa bye bye.

ON THE NATURE & HABIT OF ANTS

The ants are busy
errand-running — on twig, off twig — always
one more. It's a different life

again, antenna-led, six-wheel-drive — let no
more heartsore human envy
their strength to weight ratio but consider

the molten glass
of their logic, the way
they know, by the density of shadows,

where they are, and what to do — when to fear, flee, fight,
by the strummings
of the land's magnetism; the way they care

not for the dated infrastructure of pine-needles, & less
for the wind's whimsical engineering; or how
in clouds, rain, or deepest

moon-bone night, they navigate
the pigtails of the dark, manipulating
the ground's sentiments; how, in this metropolis

of lichen-splotched quartzite,
they travel by the gaze
of the screech owl; how their hearts pump mercury;

how they are as rambunctious
on the tongue, & diverse,
as buzzard spleen.

SKINK

I watched you
change colors in the Florida sun.
Your quickness blistered me,
the throb in your jowl,
how your toes clung to wall and screen alike.
But then your tail was my youth
and I wanted it. Some kind of cave
collapsed in me. I saw
the day-glo newts
that saved me in the woods
where I tried to die.
I saw the hellbender, which I've looked for,
looked for, and never seen,
and the dusky and spotted salamanders.
At once it seemed you were the handwriting
on a document I'd have read to me
by some official of the government, or doctor,
the fine print. I saw you
look at my daughter each time
she sighed, and did not offer her to you.
It was clear that the darts
in your skull were the same as my father's,
and mine. Resemblances,
so what. I did not begrudge
that later you would sleep
buried to your ears
in spanish moss. I did not even wonder,
reptile, if it would be green or red,
your tail, strung on a line
around my neck,
or just that strange, courteous yellow.

NOW THE YELLOW BREECHES

Now the Yellow Breeches,
that sweet-teaed tributary of the Susquehanna, splints the light
desire-ways, it turns —
wet supremacist —

on the soft satisfactions of silt.
Now it runs on
in rivulets, ladling
its sprawl, its trenchant vinegar

through the undercanopy,
through the fox grape and catbriar.
One fragrance, one craving, one limestone octave
after another,

the Yellow Breeches blossoms
against the cement retaining wall,
foamlicked & fungal, a few
long stones, underneath,

transomed, as if a reflection
of the south bank, where
trees divide field from spackled sky, where ducks
on the mud-slick berm prance

leary & awkward
in their orange boots. Mercy
how the Yellow Breeches urges its lips
against the elder's garnet plumage,

how it savors, how it enchants,
its tongue maternal and humungous
with glee; mercy, Lord
have mercy, how it slivers past,

how the Yellow Breeches
sands down its keel, bevels
and wraps its ribs around answers
nobody's found the question for.